Ansel Adams

AMERICA'S PHOTOGRAPHER

Ansel Adams

AMERICA'S PHOTOGRAPHER

A biography for young people

by Beverly Gherman

LITTLE, BROWN AND COMPANY

BOSTON   NEW YORK   LONDON

I'm grateful to Amy Hsu, my diligent and patient editor; to Caitlyn Dlouhy, who passed her the torch; to Anne Adams Helms, who was generous with her family histories; to Michael and Jeanne Adams, who shared their family photographs; and to Mary Alinder, who encouraged me from the beginning.

First Edition

Acknowledgments of permission to reprint previously published material appear on pages 106–107.

ISBN 0-316-82445-3
LCCN 2002103229

10 9 8 7 6 5 4 3 2 1

Amilcare Pizzi

Printed in Italy

For Chuck, my master photographer,
and his four favorite subjects:
Zachariah and Emma,
Matthew and Benjamin

Oak Tree, Snowstorm, Yosemite, 1948

"The man who made unforgettable images out of the grandeur and mystery of nature did so because he could not help doing so, because he loved what he saw. The man who spent his energy defending nature against the careless and greedy also worked from love."

—WALLACE STEGNER, November 1987

Contents

Visualization

* * *

Ansel Adams's favorite place was on top of mountains. His favorite peak was Half Dome, the mountain sharply sliced down the middle. He said it was "never the *same* Half Dome, never the same light or the same mood."

One April morning in 1927, Ansel, his fiancée, Virginia, and two friends set out early to photograph Half Dome.

Ansel carried a heavy camera pack weighing at least forty pounds. It held his 6½ x 8½–inch Korona view camera, lenses, and twelve glass plates. He also had a heavy wooden tripod attached to the pack. In those days he could "climb thousands of feet with a heavy pack and think nothing of it." It helped that Ansel, at twenty-five, was tall, skinny as a rail, and quite fit. Fortunately all four of them were strong climbers, because this was a steep, snowy hike.

As they continued up the rugged peaks, Ansel stopped to take pictures. He photographed Mount Clark, Yosemite Valley, and Virginia, who was almost invisible against the powerful landscape surrounding her.

At last they reached the Diving Board, a broad granite slab four thousand feet above the valley. Ansel hoped to capture Half Dome from that perch.

It was almost noon. When he peered through his camera, he saw that Half Dome was still in shadow. He suggested they eat lunch and wait for the sun to

Opposite: *Half Dome, Apple Orchard, Winter, Yosemite National Park, circa 1930*

touch Half Dome. By mid-afternoon the light seemed right. He had only two glass plates left. He put one of them into the film holder, took the picture, and knew he had not captured the "staggering view of Half Dome" he was searching for. The peak was still half in shadow and half in light, and that was not the result he wanted.

Now he had only a single plate left. He set up the camera and suddenly decided to use a red filter to darken the sky and accentuate the brightness of the peak. He covered the camera and slipped under his camera cloth. Again he took the picture. He carefully wrapped the glass plate with his camera cover, and added it to his pack so that all of the plates were protected and would not break against each other.

Back in the darkroom, he was excited when he took the last glass plate from the fixing bath. There was Half Dome against a darkened sky, as powerful as the emotional image he had visualized. He called the image *Monolith,* and it became one of his most important photographs. The startling idea of using a red filter at just the right moment was a breakthrough for him. It produced a photograph that represented an emotional response one might have when hearing a powerful piece of music or poetry or prose. It was like no image he had created before, and it made him wonder whether he might yet pursue a career in photography.

But no, he reminded himself, he was preparing to become a classical pianist, not a photographer.

Monolith, The Face of Half Dome, Yosemite National Park, California, 1927

CHAPTER 1

Broken Nose, High Spirit

* * *

NSEL ADAMS WAS BORN on February 20, 1902, in his family's San Francisco flat on Maple Street. His father, Charles Hitchcock Adams, had attended the University of California at Berkeley, where astronomy was his favorite subject. After two years he had to leave school to help with his family's lumber business.

Like most women of the time, Ansel's mother, Olive Bray Adams, did not have a university education. However, she loved poetry, especially that of Robert Browning and Elizabeth Barrett Browning. She also played the piano and painted china.

In 1903, Charles paid nine hundred dollars for three lots on the sand dunes at the western edge of San Francisco. He wanted his family to live near healthy ocean air. On the middle lot he built a sturdy home, and on the adjoining lots he planted gardens. Olive carried baby Ansel up the steps when the three of them moved into the house in April of 1903.

Even before he could walk, Ansel Adams looked carefully at the world. From his baby carriage he

Adams family house, San Francisco, 1903 (Charles Adams)

Opposite: *Leaves, Screen Subject, Mills College, California, circa 1931*

Ansel at eight months, 1902

watched the fog silently and slowly erase the blue sky over his head. From his father's arms, during a party, he squinted against the brightness of the chandelier and its glaring reflections around the room. They were too sharp for his sensitive eyes. As a small boy, Ansel listened to the pounding surf through the open windows and watched the small fishing boats rise and fall like toys on the ocean waves. Ansel also watched the changing light on the water, how it darkened during a storm, and turned brilliant magenta with the setting sun or foamy white as the waves broke against the rocks. The setting of the house, so close to the Pacific Ocean, gave Ansel the perfect vantage point for observing the natural world, even before he could explore it for himself.

He soon learned that nature was not always predictable. Four-year-old Ansel and his elderly nanny, Nelly, shared a room. Around five in the morning on April 18, 1906, Ansel and Nelly were jolted awake by a major earthquake. Their beds were thrown about like boats on a stormy ocean. They heard the terrible crash of the brick chimney as it landed on the glass greenhouse Ansel's father had built.

His mother rushed to their room and found Nelly and Ansel grasping each other. She described how the fireplace in her room had also collapsed and left a hole in the wall. The three of them cautiously made their way downstairs, where they found broken pottery, crushed jars of preserves, floors covered with plaster, and another destroyed fireplace in the living room.

Mr. Kong, the family's Chinese cook, moved the wood-burning stove outside the house, where he was able to prepare breakfast once he found undamaged food. There were constant aftershocks to worry them, none so strong as the original earthquake, which measured 8.3 on the Richter scale, yet strong enough to cause the ground to vibrate.

While the adults were making order inside the house, Ansel was curious to see what had happened in the garden. A sharp aftershock threw him against a brick wall, where he struck his nose. It wouldn't stop bleeding, even though his mother kept putting cold packs on it. She saw how crooked and swollen it looked and thought it must be broken. The doctor agreed, but said it would be best to do nothing about straightening Ansel's nose until he matured. Ansel went through life with his nose "pointing violently to the left" and liked to joke that he never did mature.

The days after the 1906 earthquake were confusing for everyone, especially a four-year-old boy. It was Ansel's first realization that he was not totally safe, even in his own home. There were dangers that his parents could not prevent.

Soldiers from the nearby Presidio military reservation brought the family fresh water. The army and local police tried to keep law and order all over San Francisco. There was a terrible fire in the eastern part of town, including what was known as Chinatown. Mr. Kong never found his family, and was certain they had all died in that fire.

Charles was in Washington, D.C., at the time of the earthquake. Olive could not reach her husband there. Charles could not reach his family in San Francisco. All he knew from newspaper reports was that the city was burning, and that made him more fearful about what had happened to them. As soon as he could get a seat he took a train across the country, arriving in San Francisco nearly a week later.

First he had to get a special pass from the martial-law authorities to enter the city. Then without streetcars or other transportation available, he was forced to walk almost seven miles from one end of San Francisco to the other. He saw people living in the parks and on the streets. He saw the skeletons of

Children in refugee camp after San Francisco earthquake, 1906

homes left exposed when their walls had crumpled, and stairways that led nowhere. Once he reached home at the edge of the ocean, he was relieved to find his household safe and the house still standing.

Fortunately, the house had been built of the finest lumber from the family's lumber company and had therefore withstood the intense shaking of the earthquake. When things calmed down, Charles found workmen and supplies to repair the damaged chimneys and walls of the house.

It took a year for a clockmaker to repair the family's grandfather clock, which had toppled over and slid across the living room, its wooden gears and shaft scattered nearby. Ansel studied the many parts carefully. Already he was fascinated by instruments — by his father's telescope, by the surveyor's transit and telescope when the nearby area was divided for lots.

It was lucky for Ansel that the earthquake did not make his parents fearful for his safety as he grew up. They allowed him great freedom to explore the sand dunes surrounding their home. In nearby Lobos Creek he found minnows, tadpoles, water bugs, and dragonflies. He climbed the cliffs and rocks surrounding the creek and brought home interesting insects to be killed and pinned for his collection. When one of his aunts came to visit she found bugs in his bureau drawer and was terrified they might rise from their pins and begin crawling all over her room.

Ansel tried to play games like chess and cribbage and pinochle with his father, but it was too hard for him to sit still. He tried roller-skating, but found

Dunes near the Adamses' house, San Francisco, circa 1917

that he often fell or had "close calls with automobiles and horses." He decided that running was his favorite way to get around. He ran to do errands for his mother or for the pleasure of running itself. No matter how far he ran during the day, he always returned to his sand dunes in the afternoon to search for more creatures and to watch the passing ships if the day were clear. When the fog came in, he listened to the music of the foghorns as if they were his friends.

He always insisted that this early environment shaped his life — the sights, the sounds, the smells of his world. He didn't know what would have become of him if he had not been born near the ocean.

+ + +

ANSEL CALLED his father Carlie or Pop. Carlie called him Ants. The two of them walked across the sand dunes surrounding their home to study the view. Carlie pointed out where the Pacific Ocean narrowed into the waters of the San Francisco Bay. The entrance, called the Golden Gate, gave them a long, uninterrupted view of the bay and its islands. In the future, the Golden Gate Bridge would join San Francisco and Marin across the narrows.

Golden Gate before the Bridge, San Francisco, California, 1932

Grandfather Adams's lumber business failed after there were mill fires and shipwrecks combined with the economic depression. A chemical company Carlie formed with Ansel's uncle, Ansel Easton, and a friend also came to financial ruin.

Carlie was forced to take jobs as an insurance salesman and then as a business manager for the Merchant's Exchange in downtown San Francisco. It was a comedown for him; Olive and her family never let him forget it.

By 1907, Olive's father and sister were penniless and could no longer support themselves in Nevada. They came to live with Ansel's parents in San Francisco. When the three of them found fault with Carlie, Ansel was troubled and tried to defend his father.

Grandfather Bray was not used to young children, and he was often startled by Ansel's many questions. When Ansel once asked, "Does God go to the toilet?" his grandfather shouted with displeasure, "Plague be gone, young'un!"

Aunt Mary was not as strict or easily shocked as her father. She encouraged Ansel to read and stretch his mind. But she definitely sided with his mother over what they both considered his father's financial downfall.

Ansel and his father spent long evenings together studying the sky, locating their favorite constellations, and avoiding the disapproval Ansel's mother and her family expressed toward Carlie. Father and son were good friends, and although Ansel was only eleven, he sympathized with his father's financial difficulties.

Grandfather Bray, Ansel's mother, Aunt Mary, and Ansel's father in the Adamses' living room, circa 1918

CHAPTER 2

Too Active for School

* * *

ANSEL WAS NOT A HANDSOME CHILD. With dark circles under his eyes, a crooked nose, and large ears, he looked like a squirrel. The other kids teased him about his looks and the fact that he was always moving and talking. Today he would be called hyperactive and there would be some understanding of his problem. In those days the teachers wanted him to sit quietly and not cause trouble.

At age nine he went to the nearby Rochambeau School, which seemed to him extremely brown: the building, the walls, even the atmosphere. Beasley, the school bully, always tried to beat him up, but one day Ansel got so mad he swung wildly and knocked Beasley out. The principal walked Ansel home and told his mother that fighting was not allowed at school. Secretly, Ansel was pleased that he had not been afraid to fight.

He felt trapped in the classroom, listening to the foghorns, wishing he could be outside. He couldn't memorize the states or remember the rules of grammar. He wanted to run outdoors. When he could stand it no longer, he yelled at his teacher and was escorted home again. Carlie decided not to find another school. He would teach Ansel at home — French, algebra, and the English classics. Aunt Mary would share her knowledge of books. Greek, Ansel

Ansel at eleven, 1913

Opposite: *Redwoods in Fog, Bohemian Grove, California, 1963*

Rocks, Baker Beach, San Francisco, California, circa 1931

would learn from a local minister, who added lessons about faith and religion until Ansel said he was an agnostic unable to accept the minister's ideas if they did not include theories of evolution and science.

When he was twelve, Ansel started picking out notes on the piano on his own. Then his neighbor, Henry Cowell, came over to play on Ansel's piano and made the old upright sing. Henry was sixteen, and Ansel was impressed. He wanted to learn to play like that. His mother bought him piano music, and Ansel taught himself to read and memorize the notes. When Carlie saw how quickly Ansel was learning, he suggested he and Olive find a piano teacher for their talented son.

For the next three years, Ansel studied with three different teachers, who all agreed that he was a fine musician. He had found something he loved to do and was able to concentrate as he had never done before. At first he disliked having to practice the same scales and phrases over and over, but he soon discovered that his playing improved greatly when he worked hard. He started with the Bach inventions and then began playing more advanced music by Bach, Beethoven, and Chopin.

He played on the family's piano for eight years, but he knew that someday he would need a better instrument if he were to become a fine pianist. He visited a downtown music store whenever he could, and the salesmen let him practice on all their pianos. One day in 1923, he sat down at a new Mason and Hamlin piano. After playing only a few notes, Ansel knew this was the right piano for him. It had an exquisite tone and a delicate touch.

It also cost a fortune. Almost seven thousand dollars — more than seventy-three thousand dollars in today's money. Ansel had little money of his own, and he knew his parents could not afford to give him such a large sum. Carlie told him they would find a way. Ansel's uncle had given Ansel a piece of property in Atherton, thirty miles south of San Francisco, that could be sold to serve as a down payment on the piano. Then they arranged to pay seventy-five dollars a month for the next five years until the piano would be his.

Ansel used the money he made from giving music lessons to pay off the loan. He also contributed money to the family, even though it was a small amount. His new piano "was installed as though a queen in residence in a simple cottage."

Ansel playing the piano, circa 1922

Ansel's pass to the Panama-Pacific International Exposition, 1915

In 1915, his father gave thirteen-year-old Ansel a season ticket to the Panama-Pacific International Exposition being held in San Francisco to celebrate the rebuilding of the city after the earthquake and fire.

Carlie hoped Ansel would make the Exposition his school for the year while he continued to study literature, language, and the piano at home. Every day Ansel took the streetcar back and forth to see the exhibits in the Marina District.

In the Festival Hall he listened to the large organ, and then he ran about a mile to have lunch at the cafeteria in the YMCA. He played the piano at the Nevada Building and attended lectures in other buildings. He visited the Palace of Fine Arts to see works of art by Cézanne, Gauguin, Monet, and Van Gogh, and an exhibit of photography that included three prints by Edward Weston.

Ansel later admitted he didn't really understand the art, but he was intrigued by the vibrant colors and lush brush strokes the artists had used. At home he tried to paint a modern portrait of his father similar to those he had seen at the Exposition, and realized painting was not as easy as it seemed.

Sometimes Carlie met him at the science and machinery exhibits. Often Ansel's mother and aunt also came and stayed for dinner and the nightly fireworks.

Ansel volunteered to demonstrate the huge Adding Machine at one exhibit. He frequently visited the Underwood Typewriter exhibit, which presented the history of office writing and had the latest typewriter of 1915, as well as a giant-sized model of a typewriter.

In the amusement park, called the Zone, he often rode the roller coaster, the carousel, and the Aeroscope, a ride that rose three hundred feet into the air and let him see the whole Exposition from on high.

On the last evening of the Exposition, Ansel ate an enormous meal of turkey and dressing and ice cream. Shortly afterward he decided to ride the roller coaster one last time. With all that food jiggling around in his stomach, he felt so sick he had to go to the infirmary, where the nurse checked him over and suggested he rest for a time. Once he felt better, he decided to start for home and was caught in the enormous rush of the crowd as everyone was leaving.

He found the streetcar packed so tightly that there wasn't room for even one more person, so he began slowly walking the four miles home, stopping frequently because his stomach was still upset. He knew his family, waiting at home for him, must be worried, but he couldn't go any faster. It grew later and later, and still he was far from home. He imagined his parents getting up to peer out the windows in search of him. Finally, just as the grandfather clock struck two in the morning, Ansel arrived home. He was exhausted, but extremely happy. He told his parents he'd had a terrific year. No stomachache could spoil that!

The Exposition had given Ansel a sense of the world beyond San Francisco — its science, art, and entertainment. He participated in the exhibits and learned how they worked, which satisfied his enormous curiosity. He met people who thought he had a good mind when they heard his questions.

Constructing the Aeroscope at the Panama-Pacific Exposition, 1915

Car transporting the public through the Exposition grounds, 1915

After the Exposition ended, Ansel tried going back to several schools without success. Finally, his father arranged with Mrs. Kate Wilkins to give Ansel a signed diploma indicating that he had completed the eighth grade at her school. Ansel jokingly hung his diploma in the bathroom! Years

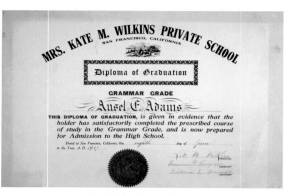

Ansel's eighth-grade diploma

later he received honorary doctorates from Harvard, Yale, the University of California at Berkeley, and other universities for his artistic and environmental contributions to the world. Those he proudly displayed in his office.

Ansel thought his father had been wise in not forcing him to sit in a class-room when it was an unnatural place for him to be. Instead Carlie found places where Ansel could stretch his mind and gain valuable knowledge.

Thundercloud, Ellery Lake, High Sierra, California, 1934

CHAPTER 3

"If, If, If!"

✴ ✴ ✴

W̲HEN A̲NSEL WAS TWELVE, he came down with measles. As the doctor advised, his mother sent him to bed in a darkened room so that his eyes would not be hurt by bright light, and she cautioned him not to scratch his rash. She and Aunt Mary took care of all his needs during the day, and Carlie read to him in the evening when he returned from work.

Ansel knew he was not supposed to be using his eyes, but he couldn't help himself. There was too much to see in his room. He discovered a slim crack of light coming in between the shade and the top of the window. From the light through that narrow space Ansel could see the world on his ceiling, as he soon would see it through the lens of a camera. He learned that the crack was creating a situation similar to what happened when you looked through a *camera obscura,* a darkened box showing an upside-down image.

Once Ansel was over the measles, his father showed him the inside of his camera so that he could understand the concept he had seen in his room.

T̲WO YEARS LATER, Ansel was in bed with a bad cold, but this time he didn't have to protect his eyes. Aunt Mary brought him some of her books to read. He was delighted by her copy of *In the Heart of the Sierras,* by J. M. Hutchings.

Illustration of a man using a portable camera obscura to trace an image projected from the outside world. The image is reflected from the outside to a mirror located at A, then passed through B down onto the tracing paper at C.

Opposite: *Bishops Pass, Kings River Canyon, 1936*

Tenaya Lake, Mount Conness, Yosemite National Park, California, circa 1946

He read and reread the pages describing the mountains and valleys of Yosemite, and knew he had to see this wondrous place for himself. He begged his parents to plan the family's vacation there. No, they said. They preferred to go to Santa Cruz or some other nearby place. They knew nothing about Yosemite and mountains except that they thought it was difficult to get there. Aunt Mary said she could not go anywhere. She needed to stay home and care for her cat, Blinkers.

Ansel did not give up. He kept showing his mother the Yosemite photographs and told her about the Ahwahneeches, Native American tribes who had lived there for hundreds of years. He read descriptions to his father of the many powerful waterfalls and told him how bright the stars would look at night away from city lights. His parents finally gave in.

On June 1, 1916, the three of them took the Southern Pacific train from Oakland. They passed through the San Joaquin Valley with its clear skies and lush crops as far as the eye could see. They transferred to the Yosemite Valley Railroad after having lunch at a hotel in Merced.

The train was uncomfortably hot, and the family was dressed in heavy clothing for the cold days they expected to find in the mountains. Ansel's mother, ever proper in her dress and behavior, gave him and his father permission to remove their heavy jackets, but she could not possibly remove any of her many layers of clothing, including her buttoned blouse, long skirt, bloomers, khaki hat, and high boots. She had to suffer in silence.

The green, irrigated land turned to dry, golden hills of grass as they rose into the foothills and followed the Merced River with pine trees along its banks. They stayed overnight at the luxurious Del Portal Hotel. Ansel woke at dawn, not at all interested in the lush surroundings but eager to get moving on the last leg of their journey. He wanted to be in the mountains he had seen in Aunt Mary's book.

Finally the three of them were settled on an open bus, bumping along rough, unpaved roads, rising "two thousand feet in ten miles." The bus rounded curve after curve before coming to stop at Valley View.

The Adamses were covered with dust from the roads, but suddenly it didn't matter at all, especially to Ansel. They were surrounded by breathtaking views.

Ansel holding his Box Brownie camera, Yosemite National Park, circa 1918

If Ansel turned his head one way, he saw the imposing granite mountain called El Capitan. If he turned another way, he saw the rushing spray of Bridal Veil Falls. And in the distance, he saw Half Dome, a mountain looking as though it had been sliced down the middle, just as his book described. He was overcome by awe.

He realized that reading about the sights had not done them justice. Nor had the blurry photographs in the book. Nothing compared with actually seeing them. "One wonder after another descended upon us," he wrote later.

Ansel's parents surprised him with a camera — a simple Kodak Box Brownie — and he could hardly wait to take pictures of the mountains and the falls all around him. He didn't know where to begin. Should he climb up the heights or race through the meadows? Which rocks would give the best view of a waterfall?

Ansel shot one amazing sight after another. He wrote to Aunt Mary from Yosemite and sent her two pictures of Yosemite Valley. "Films are expensive to develop and I expect to be broke if I keep up the rate I am taking pictures. I have taken 30 already," he wrote.

To get a better view of Half Dome, he climbed a small tree stump near their tent. The stump crumbled beneath him, and he fell headfirst onto the ground, accidentally pushing the shutter of his box camera. Fortunately he landed on soft pine needles and didn't hurt himself or the camera.

Album page of Ansel's first photographs, Yosemite National Park, 1916 (titles are in his mother's handwriting)

When Ansel had the roll of film developed in Yosemite, Mr. Pillsbury, a local photographer, was puzzled by the upside-down image of Half Dome he found on the roll of film. He presented Ansel with the uncut negatives and asked what had happened. Although he had taken it in such an unusual way, Ansel thought it was fairly good for a beginner's photograph. But he realized that none of his prints were as powerful as the sights he had seen.

Half Dome and Clouds (Upside-down Photograph), Yosemite National Park, 1916

The next two summers Ansel went back to Yosemite, first with his mother and Aunt Mary and then by himself. He took many pictures of wildflowers to send back to his father, who loved flowers of all kinds.

In the spring of 1919, Ansel was sick again. This time he came down with the same influenza that was killing millions of people in a worldwide pandemic. He was forced to spend several weeks in bed and felt depressed that he was so weak. Once he felt a little better, he said he had to go back to Yosemite. His father thought it would lift his spirits and reserved the tent cabin at Camp Curry where they had stayed before. He asked the hostess, Mrs. Curry, to watch over Ansel.

Ansel could barely move when he arrived at Camp Curry, but within a few days he was able to hike to his favorite spots, and by the following week he had climbed Half Dome. "Yosemite cured me!" he later insisted.

Entrance to Camp Curry, Yosemite National Park

He also found a family friend, Francis Holman, whom he had met in Yosemite two years earlier. Ansel called him Uncle Frank. Uncle Frank was a retired engineer who knew the mountains well and collected birds for the San

Francisco Academy of Sciences for research, even though it saddened him to kill any creature. Uncle Frank taught Ansel how to climb and how to carry the least amount of equipment necessary.

LeConte Memorial Lodge, Yosemite National Park, circa 1923

That summer seventeen-year-old Ansel joined the Sierra Club, so that he could apply for the job of custodian of the LeConte Memorial Lodge, the small building that served as the Sierra Club's headquarters in Yosemite.

It was built as a memorial to Joseph LeConte, the great geologist and conservationist, who had died in 1901. Uncle Frank had served as custodian in previous years and thought it a perfect job for Ansel.

The previous custodian was not returning, so Ansel was hired to begin work in April of 1920. Early spring was still damp in Yosemite. Ansel found the stone cottage in terrible condition when he arrived. All the firewood was gone; everything was in disarray. It took him ten days to clean inside and out. It rained frequently and the roof leaked, so he set out buckets to catch the drips. He slept on a cot and tried to avoid the leaking roof. Once the weather warmed up he was happy to be able to sleep outside under the stars.

He straightened out all the Sierra Club material in the cottage so the members could use the books, maps, photo albums, and Club bulletins. He answered questions from hikers who stopped by and often led groups of visitors to see the many breathtaking views high above the valley. He worked hard for the small salary he was paid, and he believed in what the Sierra Club stood for — preserving and exploring the vast mountains and valleys of the Sierra range.

He and Uncle Frank planned a long trip into the High Sierra that summer. They were going to Merced Lake, Mount Clark, and the wilderness area east of the Merced Range.

Ansel wired his father to say that he needed to buy a burro to carry his camping gear and food.

CAN BUY BURRO FOR TWENTY INCLUDING OUTFIT.
CAN SELL AT END OF SEASON FOR TEN. FINE INVESTMENT
AND USEFUL. WIRE IMMEDIATELY AS OFFER IS FOR
TODAY ONLY.

His father said yes and Ansel bought the burro, named Mistletoe. When Ansel asked the park ranger what to feed the burro, the ranger told Ansel to make sure Mistletoe had plenty of water and barley. Ansel bought a box of refined pearl barley from the small local store, but Mistletoe sniffed the grain and walked away. The ranger howled with laughter when Ansel told him what he had done. He suggested Ansel get a sack of rough barley from the stables. That's what burros like. Not the pearl barley people cook in their soup. After that, the rangers called him "Pearl Barley" Adams.

Ansel and Uncle Frank each packed their burros with one hundred pounds of equipment and food.

Ansel with Mistletoe

They also carried packs on their backs weighing about thirty pounds each. From the beginning, Ansel's pack was filled with photographic equipment.

They started by taking the Sunrise Trail to Merced Lake. Ansel took many photographs of Merced Peak and Mount Clark as they explored the area for several days before returning to the LeConte Lodge. After that first experience, Ansel often went by himself to explore other areas in the Sierra. He said that he was trying to "make a visual diary" of the sights he visited.

Ansel later wrote, "How different my life would have been if it were not for these early hikes in the Sierra — if I had not experienced that memorable first trip to Yosemite — if I had not been raised by the ocean — if, if if! Everything I have done or felt has been in some way influenced by the impact of the Natural Scene. . . . I *knew* my destiny when I first experienced Yosemite."

Upper Yosemite Fall, Yosemite Valley, 1946

CHAPTER 4

In and Out of the Darkroom

* * *

AFTER SPENDING TWO SUMMERS taking photographs in Yosemite, Ansel was eager to learn how to make his own prints. He asked one of his neighbors, Frank Dittman, if he could work in his photo-finishing business. Mr. Dittman agreed to teach Ansel how to develop film if Ansel would deliver the finished snapshots to drugstores all around San Francisco. As soon as Ansel finished his deliveries, he rushed back to work in the basement darkroom with Mr. Dittman, who nicknamed him "Yosemite" because he talked endlessly about his favorite place. Mr. Dittman quickly recognized that the work came naturally to Ansel. "I could see right off he was good," Mr. Dittman later said.

Mr. Dittman taught Ansel two basic techniques: how to develop new rolls of film and how to make prints from the negatives. The experience Ansel gained in Mr. Dittman's darkroom when he was a teenager would be valuable later when he set up his own darkroom. He was so meticulous about keeping his equipment and chemicals clean that a friend said, "Ansel's darkroom could have been a surgery," because it was so neat and spotless.

Years later Ansel wrote that developing photographs was a combination of "pure science, pure witchcraft, and wishful thinking....Weird mumbo jumbo persists and flourishes." It is very complicated to produce a print from

Opposite: *Self-Portrait, Monument Valley, Utah, 1958*

a negative. There are many different types of chemicals, paper, and equipment available, and photographers have different methods of using them.

Ansel wrote a series of books that have become world famous as guides to photographic technique. They are not easy to understand, but he includes illustrations showing how the results vary according to the methods used. He was adamant that making the prints was as important as snapping the shutter.

1

2

3

Ansel experimented with the many factors involved in creating a print in order to get the results he wanted. Here, changing the agitation during negative development produced different tones and contrasts. Negative 1 is the best one to use for printing.

Based on his experience with music, he believed that "Photographers are, in a sense, composers, and the negatives are their scores."

IN JUNE OF 1920, he described in a letter to his father what he had been trying to achieve when he took a photo of Diamond Cascade in Yosemite's Tenaya Canyon. He wrote that he had the idea for the shot in his head several days before. He wanted "to interpret the power of falling water, the light and airy manner of the spray particles and the glimmer of sunlit water."

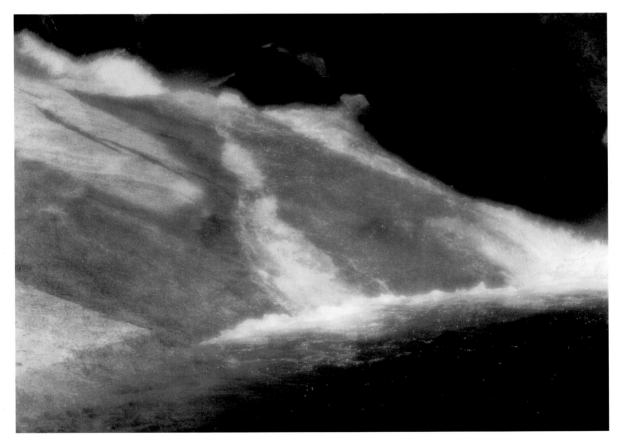

Diamond Cascade, Yosemite National Park, circa 1920

By the time Ansel took the photograph *Monolith, The Face of Half Dome* in 1927, he had changed the course of his career and the history of photography. No wonder he called it a "moment of wonder." He had been able to visualize the emotion he felt about the mountain. He emphasized that he was not trying to duplicate reality, but to make a work of art.

Half Dome, often called the "jewel of Yosemite," was one of the first sights Ansel experienced when he arrived in Yosemite as a boy. It had become a good friend to him over the years. He had climbed its granite walls many times, and continued to photograph it whenever he could. He never tired of seeing it. Now he had been able to express the feelings he felt for the mountain so that others could share them.

He rarely complained about the difficulties he endured to make his photographs, such as climbing dangerous heights to reach his subjects, carrying heavy cameras and all the other equipment he needed — often weighing as much as forty pounds — and having to rely on the weather and the light when he reached his destination.

Ansel was only twelve when he first met Cedric Wright, who was already in his twenties and a fine violinist. They met again through Sierra Club outings and became the best of friends. In 1923, Cedric introduced him to Albert Bender, who owned an insurance firm in San Francisco. Albert was an art lover who generously supported young artists. After seeing Ansel's photographs he was so impressed that he suggested Ansel publish a portfolio of eighteen of his photos. He decided they would make one hundred copies at the top price of fifty dollars each. Right then and there he wrote a check for five hundred dollars for ten portfolios. Then he got on the phone and called his friends, who said they would buy portfolios, sight unseen, because they trusted Albert's judgment.

Moon and Half Dome, Yosemite National Park, California, 1960

It was at a time when photography was not yet considered an art. The publisher refused to use the word "photographs" in the title of the portfolio. Instead she coined a new term — "Parmelian prints." Ansel went along with it, but he was embarrassed by the title, *Parmelian Prints of the High Sierras.* It should have read "Sierra," not "Sierras," and Ansel worried that the public would be upset by the error and by the strange name. And that no one would want to buy the portfolios. But that didn't happen. All of them were sold. It meant that Ansel's work was finding an audience and he was earning some much-needed money.

Roaring River Falls, Kings Canyon National Park, California, 1925 (from Parmelian Prints of the High Sierras)

CHAPTER 5

"Sierra Sky and Stone"

* * *

THE SIERRA CLUB WAS A VITAL PART of Ansel's life. He went on Sierra Club outings year after year. During those trips he led groups on vigorous hikes, rushed off whenever possible to take photographs, and returned to lead the evening festivities. As soon as he was home, he wrote about the trips for the Sierra Club magazine and developed the negatives he had made. To him, it was not just an organization, it was a way of life.

The Sierra Club had been founded in June of 1892 by John Muir and a small group of students and faculty members from the University of California at Berkeley. The group chose Muir to be their first president and wrote a formal statement describing their goals: "To explore, enjoy, and render accessible the mountain regions of the Pacific Coast."

Muir was an early explorer and conservationist, who once told a friend, "Won't it be wonderful when a million people can see what we are seeing?" as they stood at Glacier Point and looked out at a Yosemite Valley largely untouched by human presence. Fortunately, in 1890, Muir had persuaded President William Henry Harrison to sign a bill making Yosemite a national park and preserving its natural beauty forever.

Ansel with wooden camera and tin cup, 1930s (Cedric Wright)

Opposite: *Nevada Fall, Yosemite National Park, California, 1946*

In 1901, the Sierra Club started annual outings to introduce people to the beauty of the High Sierra. There were often two hundred members who signed up to spend two weeks or a month in the mountains. A pack train of fifty mules was required to carry supplies. Four men were in charge of meals, and two would gather wood for the stoves. It was a major challenge to feed two hundred people, three meals a day,

Hundreds of Sierra Club hikers around a campfire at Darwin Bench, 1950s (Cedric Wright)

for a whole month. Each person was given a single spoon at the beginning of the outing and expected to keep it safe. Some climbers kept it inside their sock, others drilled a hole and hung their spoon around their neck. "Literally, you are born into the Sierra Club with a steel spoon in your mouth," Ansel later wrote in one of his many articles for the *Sierra Club Bulletin.*

ANSEL'S MARVELOUS SENSE of humor surfaced often. He was always playing jokes on his friends, telling stories with sound effects and dialects, making up foolish words, and adding ridiculous finales to his piano playing to make everyone laugh. When he wore a mustache, he called it his "musenttuch it." One of his favorite things was creating what he referred to as "screwball theatrical productions" for Sierra Club trips. His play *Exhaustos, a Tragedy in the Greek Manner* was performed on the 1932 outing. The cast included roles such as King

Dehydros of Exhaustos; his daughter, Clymenextra (Climb-an-Extra), who had early flashbulbs hanging from her ears; Prince Rhycrispos; and the Chorus of Weary Men and Sunburnt Women. Ansel played the Spirit of the Itinerary, dressed in a white sheet, wearing a wreath on his head, and carrying a harp made of bent wood and fishing line. His friend Cedric hid in the bushes, producing unearthly sounds with his violin.

Cast of Exhaustos, 1932 (with Ansel as the Spirit of the Itinerary)

On other nights Cedric played classical Bach works or accompanied while others sang. Someone was always willing to tell stories or recite poetry for the group around the crackling campfire.

Cedric made sturdy wooden cases to protect his violin and camera as they were jostled on the back of a mule. He also designed clever portable latrines that he called "Straddlevariouses," as a pun on the famous Stradivarius violin.

On the 1932 outing, Ansel made a photograph he thought was one of his best. He called it *Lake and Cliffs.* Some of his viewers called it "abstract" and found it difficult to understand. Ansel said he knew what he was framing in his camera and that it was an "extract" of the scene.

Yet it is mysterious. The viewer sees layers of unusual vertical and horizontal shapes, heavy shapes resting on a silvery surface. Gradually one begins to recognize a granite peak resting on a frozen lake. A frozen lake rising up inside

Lake and Cliffs, Sierra Nevada, 1932

the peak. Rocks strewn on ice. Light slashing across the water's surface. The peaks reflected upside down in the dark water. And then it makes sense. Ansel has photographed only the base of Eagle Scout Peak and a portion of the frozen Precipice Lake.

ANSEL WROTE about his outings for the *Sierra Club Bulletin:* "No matter how sophisticated you may be, a large granite mountain cannot be denied — it speaks in silence to the very core of your being.... You were aware of Sierra sky and stone, and of the emerald splendor of Sierra forests."

Over the years Sierra Club outings had to change in a way John Muir could not have anticipated. In order to preserve wilderness areas, large numbers of mules could no longer be allowed along the trails. No longer were nightly campfires safe, nor could branches be used for cooking fires. Instead propane was packed, the number of people was severely limited, and the Sierra Club was forced to rewrite its goals: "To explore, enjoy, and preserve" rather than "render accessible."

Ansel was relieved, because he was aware of how fragile the land was every time he set out on a Sierra Club outing.

CHAPTER 6

Marriage in the Mountains

✳ ✳ ✳

By the 1920s, Ansel had found a good routine for his life. He spent his summers in Yosemite, hiking, climbing, and taking photographs. The rest of the year he lived in San Francisco, concentrating on his music. Because he intended to earn his living as a classical pianist, he knew he couldn't take three summer months away from practicing while he was in the mountains, so he began to search for a piano in the Yosemite area. Friends mentioned that a local man named Harry Best kept an old Chickering piano in his painting studio. He also sold his paintings of Yosemite and other souvenir items there.

"I was first attracted to Mr. Best's piano and soon thereafter to his seventeen-year-old daughter," Ansel later wrote. Virginia Best lived in Yosemite and took care of things for her father after her mother's death. Virginia was planning a career as a classical singer. Ansel and Virginia found they shared many interests, including music and their love for Yosemite.

Virginia Rose Best and Merced River, Yosemite National Park, circa 1921

Opposite: *Two Dead Trees Against Black Sky, Sierra Nevada, 1925*

During a long wilderness hike Ansel wrote to Virginia, "As soon as I am back in Yosemite, I shall make a beeline for Best's Studio" to practice the piano. He hoped Virginia would read between the lines and realize that he was also looking forward to seeing her. They continued to write each other when Ansel returned to San Francisco.

The following summer, when Ansel was again in Yosemite, he wrote to his father that he had "met someone, whom I have grown very fond of indeed.... The world seems fuller, more beautiful — there is something in it now that was not there before....She constantly reminds me of my mother — more so every day — by her kindness, gentleness, and good level head." Yet Ansel didn't want his parents to think that he would no longer care about them. "Remember this," he wrote, "my first duty is to you and my mother."

He invited Virginia to meet his parents early in the fall of 1923. He told her that he was working hard on his music and would think of photography as only a hobby and an opportunity to earn extra money until he was able to support them with his music. But again he showed his ambivalence when he went on in great detail to explain that he would do only the very best prints he could, using the finest materials.

He also didn't rush to set a wedding date. Instead he and Virginia continued to see each other when he was in Yosemite and to correspond when they were apart.

In November of 1923, he wrote Virginia telling her that he had to reconsider their relationship. He needed to earn a living and help his aging parents. That was his first responsibility. He suggested it would be wiser if they began seeing other people. Cedric Wright had introduced him to many other young men and women who loved music and books, and Ansel was interested in broadening his circle of friends.

He and Virginia continued to write each other, and Ansel used his letters to advise Virginia on how she should spend her time: "Promise me, dear, that you will work with all your heart and soul with your voice, and that you will devote much of your spare time to cultural subjects." In his letters he sounded more like a father than a friend or lover. In fact, he sounded like his own father, who continued to give him sound advice whenever he wrote or talked to Ansel.

Ansel soon discovered that the other young women he met were not able to tolerate his intense personality. Meanwhile, Virginia waited patiently for him to realize that she was the right one for him.

Ansel finally came to the same conclusion, and on New Year's Eve of 1927, he proposed to her. Virginia said yes. They set the wedding date for two days later, because she did not want to wait a moment longer. After all, it had been a long courtship; they had been "engaged-disengaged-reengaged" during the previous six years.

On January 2, 1928, they had a small wedding in Yosemite with only their families and a few friends present. There was no time for Virginia to buy a wedding dress, so she wore her best dress, even though it was black, and Ansel wore his knickers and basketball shoes!

After their wedding, the young couple lived part of the time with Ansel's parents in San Francisco and the rest of the time in Yosemite with Virginia's father.

Ansel and Virginia on their wedding day

Their first child was born in Yosemite on August 1, 1933, while Ansel was leading a Sierra Club outing in the High Sierra. He rushed back early, but Michael had been born even earlier. On March 8, 1935, Anne also arrived earlier than expected, so Ansel missed her birth, too.

In 1936, when both children were quite small, Harry Best died,

Ansel measuring photographs of Yosemite with Michael looking on, circa 1935

and Virginia became the owner of Best's Studio. She and Ansel decided to carry fine books and authentic Native American crafts in the shop, not just mass-produced souvenirs. The National Park Service had other ideas. When the Service refused to let Best's publish and sell material, the couple decided to establish Five Associates, which would publish photographic postcards, note cards, picture books, and guidebooks for the area. Ansel also had some of his negatives printed by an assistant and sold them as 8 x 10–inch Special Edition prints.

Michael and Anne grew up in the beautiful surroundings of Yosemite, attending the local grammar school only a short walk away. They even became "celebrities" in the 1940s when their parents produced a children's book about their activities. Called *Michael and Anne in the Yosemite Valley,* the book was a great favorite of park visitors. When Ansel traveled for photographic assignments, Virginia stayed behind with the children. Several times he took Anne or

Michael with him on a trip, but most of the time they were involved in school and activities with their friends.

Michael went to Wasatch Academy in Utah for high school, and then to Stanford University. Anne went to Dominican High School in San Rafael before she attended Barnard and Stanford.

Despite the distance, Yosemite would continue to be a magnet for Anne and Michael, as it had always been for their parents.

Anne, Virginia, and Michael, circa 1941

CHAPTER 7

To Play or Not to Play

* * *

*I*N THE SPRING OF 1930, Ansel and Virginia built a home next door to his parents, on the lot that had been his mother's dahlia garden. It was designed as a studio for Ansel's music and his photography, with a high ceiling to provide the best acoustics, and with windows to bring in the best light all through the day. Ansel had everything he needed to continue his full life.

For years he had been studying to become a concert pianist. At the same time, he had been perfecting his technique as a photographer. He wanted to continue doing both, but it was getting more difficult to juggle two demanding professions. Playing the piano meant practicing long hours every day. The kind of photography Ansel wanted to do required him to travel, either to Yosemite or to the Southwest, and also meant long hours in the darkroom.

There were not enough hours in his day. The strain was beginning to show. He knew he had to choose between the piano and the camera. His father urged him not to rush his decision, even if it took twenty-five years! He wanted Ansel to love the work he chose to do, because he himself was so unhappy stuck in an office doing paperwork.

In the summer of 1930, Ansel returned to New Mexico to complete the Taos Pueblo photographs he was taking of the adobe houses and the men and

Opposite: *Eagle Dance, San Ildefonso Pueblo, New Mexico, 1928–29*

Aspens, Dawn, Dolores River Canyon, Colorado, 1937

women who lived there. He had been given special permission by the Native American's to witness their sacred dancing as well as their daily activities. He was also working in collaboration with the well-known writer Mary Austin, who would create the text.

Since his first trip to the Southwest two summers before, he had been astonished by the light on the land and the sudden power of the storms. The sky seemed endless and reflected the magnificent colors of sunrise and sunset like no place he had ever seen. As it turned out, the setting and two men he met there would help him make the most important choice of his life.

Woman, Taos Pueblo, New Mexico, circa 1928

⋄ ⋄ ⋄

ANSEL HAD HOPED to stay at Mabel Dodge Luhan's estate, Los Gallos. She always had a house full of writers and artists, and this time she didn't have room for him. She asked the photographer Paul Strand and his wife to let Ansel use their extra bedroom, even though they had never met him.

At that first meeting with Paul Strand, Ansel wanted to see some of his recent work. He knew of Strand's fine reputation and admired his photographs. However, Strand had no prints to show him that day. Instead he took Ansel to the window and carefully held up his new 4 x 5–inch negatives, one by one, against a piece of white paper.

Ansel was so inspired by the power of what he saw, he knew he had to continue his work in photography. His mind was made up. His friend Albert Bender had been telling him to do this all along. "My understanding of photography was crystallized that afternoon as I realized the great potential of the medium as an expressive art." He resolved, "The camera, not the piano, would shape my destiny."

On that same trip Ansel also met watercolor painter John Marin at Los Gallos. "I shall never get out of my mind the thrill of seeing his things. It was the first great experience in Art I had," Ansel later wrote. At the Panama-Pacific Exposition years before, when Ansel was only a boy, he had seen the latest European art, but he hadn't understood it. Since then he had studied the changes in art and the development of photography. Now when he saw Marin's delicate watercolors he realized that the unpainted spaces were equally as important as the painted spaces. He watched as Marin studied the landscape, sometimes for hours, before he even started painting. And then, using a brush or even his thumb, he made just a few touches of paint to paper, and

Iris, Maine, 1928 (Paul Strand)

captured the mountains and sky with such accuracy and sensitivity that Ansel was astounded. He couldn't wait to get back to San Francisco to tell Virginia of his decision.

Virginia was pleased, but Ansel's mother was shocked. She didn't want him to give up the piano and questioned his decision. "You're not going to be just a photographer, are you?" she asked. All she knew was that photographers set up their cameras and took family photos or individual portraits. She didn't consider it an important profession compared to being a classical pianist who played concerts and received society's approval. And she was not alone. At that time photographers were not accepted by the art world, and their work was not considered fine art by museums or their patrons.

There was no way she or Carlie or anyone else in the family could anticipate how famous Ansel's photographs would become someday and that he would never be "just a photographer." They could not know that photography would be recognized as an art form as respected as oil painting, and that Ansel's images, such as *Half Dome, Winter* and *Moonrise, Hernandez,* would become well-known around the world.

In the beginning of his photography career, Ansel did not earn much money. He took on as many projects as he could so that he and Virginia could pay their bills. He did commercial catalogs, portraits of famous people, wedding photographs, and pictures for ads. But he always felt under financial pressure, without enough money to get by.

One day he was asked to photograph the Chinese Baptist Kindergarten in San Francisco. In the classroom, he set up his camera on a tripod as he explained to the children what he was doing and told them where to stand. He mixed flash powder and added a little extra to make up for the dark walls inside. He chirped like a bird so that the children would look at him, put his head under the dark cloth, raised the flashgun into the air, and fired the shutter. There was an explosion in the room with so much smoke that someone called the fire department, and a fire truck sped to the school, loudly clanging its bells. It seems Ansel had used too much flash powder!

Chinese Baptist Kindergarten, San Francisco, circa 1920

When the smoke cleared, Ansel found the children hiding under their desks. He coaxed them out and led them to the schoolyard, where he took a picture without any flash powder at all. Such accidents were avoided later, in the 1930s, when flashbulbs were invented.

IN 1932, Ansel met a group of Bay Area photographers who were eager to make photographs that did not imitate other art forms. They called themselves Group *f*/64. The term stood for the lens aperture, or opening, that provided the sharpest photographs with the greatest depth of field. They did "straight photography," in contrast to the pictorialists, whom Ansel and his friends called the "fuzzy-wuzzies." He felt those photographers were continuing to imitate painting, not trying to develop a new art form. They dressed models in historical costumes and had them pose suggestively to catch the viewer's eye. Many members of Group *f*/64 had done pictorial work at some point, but now they wanted to move beyond such staged and static settings.

The director of San Francisco's M. H. de Young Memorial Museum came to a display of Group *f*/64's work and was so impressed, he offered them an exhibition at the museum. It was held in November and December of 1932 and included eighty photographs by Ansel, Imogen Cunningham, Edward Weston, his son Brett, and others. Ansel exhibited three nature photographs: *Nevada Fall, Yosemite Valley; Golden Gate before the Bridge; Lake and Cliffs*. He also included three portraits and an architectural study.

The prices for the photographs were only ten to fifteen dollars, but the public response was heated. People wrote letters of protest, saying that photographs were not art and did not deserve to be exhibited at a major museum. The director stood his ground. So did Ansel, strongly responding to letters of criticism he received.

One of the letters was from a pictorialist in Los Angeles who took pictures of models dressed to represent characters from another time. Ansel thought his work was awful and wrote back, saying, "The basic aspects of photography are so clearly defined in themselves that I am astonished you have so completely missed them."

In Golden Canyon, Death Valley, circa 1946

CHAPTER 8

First Trip East

∗ ∗ ∗

ANSEL AND VIRGINIA TRAVELED EAST for the first time in March of 1933. One of the main reasons for the trip was for Ansel to show Alfred Stieglitz his work. Ansel had seen Stieglitz's remarkable nighttime photographs of New York in rain and snow. He had read his meaningful articles about photography as art. Stieglitz was considered the expert in the field and had a small gallery in New York City where he showed the work of young artists he found promising, including Paul Strand and John Marin.

Hopeful artists brought him their portfolios, and if he found their work exceptional he encouraged and supported them, but if he didn't, he could be ruthless in his opinions. After they had become friends, Ansel affectionately called him a "tough old bird."

On March 29, after Virginia and Ansel had settled into their hotel, he took his portfolio and set out for Stieglitz's gallery, An American Place. He was nervous. What if Stieglitz did not like his photographs? He had a letter of introduction from a prominent San Francisco woman, but no scheduled appointment. Pushing his way through crowds of pedestrians and skirting garbage cans on the sidewalk made him more nervous. New York was a bustling city compared to San Francisco. The noise of traffic, with its incessant

Opposite: *Broad Street, New York City, circa 1949*

honking, didn't help. Neither did the long bread lines and the men with hunger written on their faces.

By the time Ansel reached 509 Madison Place, took the elevator to the seventeenth floor, and entered the gallery, he was a nervous wreck. But when he found himself alone in quiet, light-filled rooms he calmed down.

He heard someone rustling paper and walked into the back room, where he found Stieglitz wrapped in a black cape, studying a book.

"What do you want?" Stieglitz asked, annoyed at being disturbed.

Ansel explained that he had come to show him his prints.

"Come back at two-thirty," Stieglitz responded, abruptly dismissing him.

Ansel was so hurt by the man's rudeness, he rushed back to the hotel and told Virginia they were going to return to San Francisco immediately. Virginia reminded him that he had come all this way to show Stieglitz his work and that was what he must do.

ANSEL REALIZED she was right and reluctantly returned to An American Place that afternoon. Stieglitz seemed more genial then. He was sitting in the only chair to be found in the studio. Ansel handed him his portfolio and leaned against the radiator. He watched as the great man untied the portfolio, took out Ansel's prints, and looked carefully at each one: a leafless poplar, tall buildings, an old barn. Ansel kept trying to explain what his intention had been when he took this picture or that, but Stieglitz shushed him each time. After several minutes, Stieglitz put all of the prints back in the portfolio, tied it, and started to say something. Then he immediately took them out again, as though he needed to be sure what he had seen was real.

Alfred Stieglitz, An American Place, New York, New York, 1944

Meanwhile, steam heat began pouring out of the radiator, and Ansel had to jump up before he burned his bottom. Stieglitz wasn't paying any attention to him. He was still studying Ansel's prints. At last he returned them to the portfolio and tied the ribbons.

"You are always welcome here," Stieglitz said, adding that the photographs were "some of the finest I've ever seen." Ansel was elated. Now he could return to San Francisco and continue working with confidence. He also began a warm correspondence with Stieglitz and returned annually to show him his latest work. This close relationship would continue until Stieglitz's death in 1946.

Stieglitz's approval gave Ansel the courage to show his work to others while he was in New York and also led to a show later in 1933 at the Delphic Studio, which had exhibited Edward Weston's photos a few years earlier. Ansel's work was well received. "It is masterly stuff," a *New York Times* reporter wrote.

In 1936, Stieglitz gave Ansel a show at An American Place. Stieglitz's wife, the painter Georgia O'Keeffe, told Ansel that Stieglitz was "pretty snooty about what he put up" on the walls and that if he hung an artist's work, that said a lot. It had certainly made a difference to her own career to have Stieglitz exhibit her paintings. He even controlled who could buy a painting or a photograph and how much they should pay.

Ansel included only four landscapes in the forty-five prints that were hung. Two of those were *Clouds, Sierra Nevada, California* and *West Slope of Mount Whitney, Sierra Nevada.* Most of the prints were close details of buildings, fences, and leaves. One taken in a cemetery, *White Gravestone,* captured the coldness of the marble in contrast to the delicacy of the carved figure grieving over a young woman's death. It was the most expensive piece in the show, listed at one hundred dollars, while the others were priced at thirty dollars. Ansel was

White Gravestone, Laurel Hill Cemetery, San Francisco, California, circa 1936

pleased to see how striking his work looked hanging on the gray walls in inter-esting groupings. Nine prints were sold in the New York show, and at the same time he had a show in Chicago, which brought him further recognition.

At thirty-four, Ansel was being recognized by the critics as a photographer who knew what he was doing with a camera and who captured scenes with great clarity.

Two years later, Ansel completed a book, *Sierra Nevada: The John Muir Trail,* which included photographs of lakes, waterfalls, peaks, and even glaciers from Kings Canyon, south of Yosemite. He hoped Kings Canyon would become a national park in the future.

Ansel sent a copy of the book to Harold Ickes, United States Secretary of the Interior, who showed it to President Franklin D. Roosevelt. The President liked it so much he decided to keep it for himself, so Ansel had to send another copy to Ickes. Both President Roosevelt and Secretary Ickes were so impressed by the scenes in Ansel's handsome photographs, they managed to persuade Congress to pass the Kings Canyon National Park bill in 1940.

He also sent a copy of the book to Stieglitz. After receiving the book, Stieglitz wrote him, "You have literally taken my breath away....What perfect photography....I am an idolator of perfect workmanship of any kind. And this is truly perfect workmanship."

Now Ansel had the approval of the photographer he most admired, and he had succeeded in protecting valuable land he cherished.

Minarets and Iceberg Lake from Volcanic Ridge, Sierra Nevada, circa 1935

CHAPTER 9

Sun and Moon

✳ ✳ ✳

I N THE FALL OF 1941, Ansel and his friend Cedric Wright drove to the Southwest in search of scenes to photograph. Ansel's eight-year-old son, Michael, joined them.

One Sunday they spent a whole day in the Chama River Valley near Ghost Ranch looking for interesting sights. But by late afternoon Ansel and Cedric were frustrated and felt they had wasted their time. It was too beautiful outside, they complained. The sky was too blue and too empty to be interesting.

Driving back along Highway 84, heading toward their Santa Fe motel, Ansel looked out the car window one last time. It was nearly dusk — the time of day, shortly before sunset, when the world turns to gold. The slant of the sun strikes whatever is in sight — the trees, the land, the hills — with an unusual light.

Ansel saw the moon rising in the east, above the small town of Hernandez, just as the sun was slipping behind the mountains in the west. Rays from the sun lit up the white crosses in the tiny cemetery and atop the church, as well as the snow-

Michael, Cedric, and Ansel packing the car before their Southwest trip, Yosemite, 1941 (Virginia Adams)

Opposite: *Aspens, Northern New Mexico, 1958 (Print 1958–60)*

Thunderstorm Over the Great Plains, Near Cimarron, New Mexico, 1961

covered mountains and thick clouds covering the scene. Ansel suddenly knew he had to capture that moment.

Quickly he pulled off the road, almost landing the car in a ditch. He shouted for Cedric and Michael to help him unload the camera, the tripod, and the lenses he would need. He locked the 8 x 10–inch view camera on the tripod and attached a deep-yellow filter to darken the sky and lighten the houses and crosses. He knew there were only seconds left before the sun would disappear completely and take its glowing light with it. He reached for his exposure meter to figure out which shutter speed to use, but the meter was not there.

All three of them began searching. They looked in the case, in the car, under the car, but could not find the meter. Ansel had to calculate everything in his head, and quickly. He set the aperture at $f/32$ and then snapped the shutter button. He started to take another shot, but the sun was gone and the scene had lost its magic.

Some would say Ansel Adams had been lucky to have seen such a sight. They would call it serendipity, a fortuitous moment he could not have anticipated. Others would say that Ansel Adams was skillful. He had been able to visualize the importance of the moment, whereas another person might have blinked or turned away.

No matter what it was, Ansel Adams had an ability to recognize such moments when they occurred. Later in life he added another explanation for the success of his many photographs. "Sometimes I think I do get to places just when God's ready to have somebody click the shutter!"

He could hardly wait to return to his San Francisco darkroom to see what he had captured on film that fall day. But first he had to complete two projects in the Southwest. It would be over a month before he was able to head home.

He knew that it would require careful developing of the negative to bring the scene to life as he had visualized it in New Mexico. But he couldn't know just how difficult it would be. He made prints from that negative many times over the years, changing his printing process slightly each time, much as a writer might revise a story, improving each version, but aware that it could always be improved even more. He kept the sky light in his first versions. He gradually darkened the sky in later versions until the crosses in the churchyard and the church itself glowed. "It was not until the 1970s that I achieved a print equal to the original visualization that I still vividly recall," he wrote in his autobiography.

Moonrise, Hernandez became his most popular photograph. Throughout his career he made around 1,300 original prints of that scene. Each print required meticulous planning. He had to be as exacting and patient with every single one he made. It was similar to the methods he had learned at the piano when he had to play the "same phrase over and over until its voicing was in his head."

A few years after taking the photograph, he told a friend, "I think it one of my best." He might have added that it was one of his most challenging.

SIXTY YEARS LATER, in the spring of 2001, *Moonrise* was shown in an exhibit at the Addison Gallery of American Art in Massachusetts. It was still viewed with awe by audiences and analyzed by critics. There is a quiet stillness in the photograph — a hush, as though life has stopped for a split second. A *Boston Globe* columnist described the scene as a "braiding together of man and nature" and wrote that it was "as much about loneliness as luminosity."

This is true for many of Ansel's photographs. He brought the solitary world to his viewers as he experienced it — without hikers, picnickers, flying birds.

Whenever he was criticized for not including people in his photographs, he countered "that there were always two people in his pictures: the photographer and the viewer."

Moonrise, Hernandez, New Mexico, 1941

CHAPTER 10

Soldier at Home

* * *

WHEN THE UNITED STATES entered World War II, Ansel wanted to enlist. He wrote, "I became outraged over the deeds of the hideous Hitler regime," even though he considered himself a pacifist. But when the army refused to take him because he was nearly forty years old and had a wife and children, he searched for other ways to help. He drove servicemen around Yosemite, where they practiced maneuvers, and he taught them how to take basic photographs that could be used for training purposes. But he wanted to do more.

After Japanese armed forces attacked Pearl Harbor in December of 1941, President Roosevelt had signed Executive Order 9066, which uprooted Japanese-American families from their homes on the West Coast and sent them to relocation camps in isolated areas of the United States. The government mistakenly worried that the Japanese, even if they were citizens of the United States, might be spies who would aid the Japanese government in the war against the United States.

Ralph Merritt, one of Ansel's friends from the Sierra Club, was named director of the Manzanar Camp and asked Ansel to come to the camp and record daily life there. He hoped to show how well the people were adapting

Opposite: *Wanda Lake, near Muir Pass, Kings Canyon National Park, circa 1934*

to their new life in a faraway place. He was not able to pay Ansel, but he could give him a place to stay and food to eat. The camp was in the Owens Valley of California, three hundred miles north of Los Angeles. Ansel had to get special permission from the gasoline ration board in Yosemite for the extra gas he would need to drive back and forth from Yosemite to Manzanar.

In the fall of 1943, he traveled there for the first time and saw how well most of the families were coping. They had prepared the rocky ground, planted vegetable gardens, and established schools, sports teams, social events, and newspapers.

Ansel chose to photograph individual families in their tiny barracks rooms, where they were surrounded by homey touches. In one photograph there is a calendar on the wall, family snapshots on the table, a plant, and a bowl of fruit with a doily underneath it. The scene is neat and tidy, and the family looks healthy. What the viewer cannot see is the life the family has left behind or the barbed wire fence locking them inside the camp.

Another photograph shows a snapshot of a serviceman next to letters he has written to his sister. The scene is subtle and makes the viewer wonder. How could this young man enlist in the army to fight for the United States when the government had imprisoned his family?

Other photographers told the story differently. One of Dorothea Lange's photographs shows a Japanese grandfather with his two

Still Life, Yonemitsu Family Quarters, Manzanar Relocation Center, California, 1943

grandsons, all three of them wearing identi-
fication tags, as though they are packages
being delivered to their assigned camp.
Their plight is a poignant reminder of the
pain of that upheaval.

Ansel and Dorothea kept up a correspondence over the years and even worked
together on photographic projects. But they
had different goals for their photographs.
She was trying to bring about social change
by showing the pain people experienced.
Ansel wrote Dorothea, "I think it is just as
important to bring to people the evidence of
the beauty of the world of nature and of
man as it is to give them a document of
ugliness, squalor and despair."

Grandfather and grandchildren awaiting evacuation bus (Dorothea Lange)

Ansel found beautiful scenes surround-
ing Manzanar. He believed that such beauty "provided the internees with
crucial emotional sustenance," just as it gave him the same response. He
looked beyond the barbed wire to photograph Mount Williamson, rising over
a bleak landscape of boulders. The image he took of the mountain, combin-
ing storm clouds and sunlight, is one of beauty and serenity, without any
indication that it is viewed from an internment camp.

Dorothea was upset by the beautiful photographs Ansel made from
Manzanar. She felt he had made relocation and life at the camp seem like a
positive experience. But that was far from the truth. He said that the experience

Mount Williamson, Sierra Nevada, from Manzanar, California, circa 1944

had been "the most important thing I've done or can do." Ansel had been emotionally moved by meeting the families at Manzanar and was eager to bring their plight to the rest of society.

In a recent magazine article one former internee described Ansel as having been a "very patriotic American" who was "riding against the tide." Ansel hoped his photographs would show the public that the imprisoned Japanese-American families were exactly like their own families — they were not enemies.

Ansel combined his photographs from Manzanar with text to create a book, *Born Free and Equal,* published in late 1944. It was his first photographic essay. The photographs and text were to be exhibited at the Museum of Modern Art in New York, but the museum administration feared that people would say his exhibit was propaganda, not art. The museum changed the title from *Born Free and Equal* to *Manzanar,* and removed text that had any information about the Japanese-Americans who were serving in the U.S. armed forces. They also moved the exhibit to the museum basement, which was a terrible disappointment to Ansel.

Later he donated his negatives from the photographs to the Library of Congress, so that they would be easily accessible to students and scholars.

CHAPTER 11

Giving Back

* * *

TEACHING CAME NATURALLY to Ansel. He began by taking piano students in the years he was studying to become a serious pianist. He encouraged Virginia "to put every ounce of energy...to the perfecting" of her singing voice. He felt that a creative life was the best life. He encouraged his children to study and take school seriously, and he shared his ideas with colleagues and friends in person and in letters.

In 1940, he started teaching at the Art Center School in Los Angeles. There he developed the Zone System with Fred Archer, another photographer at the Center. It is a guide to help photographers select the black-and-white tones they want in their finished pictures. There are eleven zones from deep black at 0 to paper white at X. Ansel assured his students they would use it intuitively once they learned it. To this day, photographers still use the Zone System.

Ansel and students, 1976 Ansel Adams Yosemite Workshop (Philip Hyde)

Opposite: *Leaves on Pool, circa 1935*

Silverton, Colorado, 1951 — a diagram of exposure zones and the corresponding print tones used in Ansel's Zone System

Ansel took his students all around the city looking for scenes to photograph. One day they might go to a park, the next day to a factory or an automobile junkyard, and another day to a bustling Los Angeles neighborhood. He wanted them to search for relationships between unusual shapes, much as a poet or writer might look for contrasting ideas with which to create a meaningful work. Ansel had done that with his image of a peaceful cemetery statue against a backdrop of oil derricks. Many years later he was amused when conservationists wanted to use that photograph, because he had taken the shot for artistic reasons, not to be used for an environmental cause.

Cemetery Statue and Oil Wells, Long Beach, California, 1939

For over twenty-five years he gave summer workshops in Yosemite. He taught thousands of students in all those years, and his best advice was "Know what you're after before you begin!" He told them he always had an image in his "mind's eye" before he took a picture.

Not only did Ansel teach in a classroom setting, he wrote many technical books with detailed information about what kind of equipment photographers needed, steps on how to develop negatives, and how to improve prints. He frequently wrote essays for the Sierra Club, and produced handsome books of photographs that included the very best reproductions possible. No matter how many letters he wrote to government officials or newspaper editors promoting the preservation of wilderness areas, and no matter how many Sierra Club articles he wrote on the same issues, his books were the most persuasive documents he created.

After seeing Ansel's book *Sierra Nevada: The John Muir Trail,* the Chief of the Forest Service wrote to Ansel, saying, "These beautiful photographs certainly impress on me the value of the objectives for which you and the other members of the Sierra Club have been fighting for many years — the preservation of the natural environment of the High Sierra."

When Kings Canyon National Park was established in 1940, the head of the National Park Service wrote to Ansel, telling him that his book was the "most effective voice in the campaign" for persuading Congress to approve the park. This was the same book that Stieglitz had found so perfect when Ansel sent it to him several years before. In it were breathtaking photographs of the high mountains.

Ansel wrote to congressmen, senators, and presidents from Franklin D. Roosevelt to Jimmy Carter, urging them to protect the environment, because

Mount McKinley and Wonder Lake, Denali National Park, Alaska, 1948 (Print 1949)

he believed that "you were either for preserving the environment or against it. There was very little middle ground."

In 1946, Ansel received a Guggenheim Fellowship to study the conditions in the national parks. Without the financial support the Guggenheim provided, Ansel could not have attempted such a major project.

He started out in Death Valley, and wrote to a friend that he was taking some of the best photographs he had ever taken. He loved the desert and thought it offered many opportunities for unusual shots.

From there he went on to Arizona, Texas, New Mexico, and the Grand Canyon, photographing and writing about the conditions he found in the parks. In 1948, his fellowship was renewed. It allowed him to travel to Alaska, where he again took memorable pictures of the landscape. While there, he said he was moved by the vastness of the area and returned home committed to preserving all the areas he had visited in Alaska and in the United States.

Thanks to Ansel's persuasive talks with him, in 1976 President Gerald Ford announced that he would ask Congress to increase acreage for the national parks, recreation areas, and wildlife sanctuaries. Unfortunately the legislation did not pass, but President Ford later wrote to his successor, Jimmy Carter, recommending Ansel for a Presidential Medal of Freedom. The Medal of Freedom is given to honor artists, writers, musicians, and religious leaders who have made enormous contributions to the country.

In June of 1980, President Carter awarded Ansel the Presidential Medal of Freedom in an outdoor ceremony at the White House. Because it was a warm summer day, Ansel sweltered in his formal wool suit, wishing he had worn his usual light jacket, bolo tie, and white Stetson hat. He was photographed as

Zabriskie Point, Death Valley National Monument, California, circa 1942

the silver medal was placed around his neck. Then the president read his moving citation:

> At one with the power of the American land-
> scape, and renowned for the patient skill and
> timeless beauty of his work, photographer
> Ansel Adams has been visionary in his efforts to
> preserve this country's wild and scenic areas,
> both on film and on Earth. Drawn to the beau-
> ty of nature's monuments, he is regarded by
> environmentalists as a monument himself, and
> by photographers as a national institution.

Ansel receiving the Presidential Medal of Freedom from President Carter,
Washington, D.C., 1980

After the official ceremony, all the honorees stood together in a receiving line and were then escorted inside to have lunch in the White House. There were thirteen other honorees, including writers Eudora Welty and Tennessee Williams, opera star Beverly Sills, and Lady Bird Johnson, who was accepting a posthumous award for her husband, former President Lyndon B. Johnson.

Ansel was seated at a table next to Mrs. Johnson and her daughter Lynda Bird, who asked for Ansel's autograph and did not stop raving about his work. It could not have been a more perfect day. He would take home his medal, his citation, and the compliments of another real-life fan.

In November 1980, just before he left office, President Carter honored Ansel again by signing legislation to preserve millions of acres of wild tundra in Alaska.

Grounded Iceberg, Glacier Bay National Monument, Alaska, 1948

CHAPTER 12

"A Green Flash"

* * *

ANSEL ADAMS BEGAN HIS LIFE in a house near the Pacific Ocean in San Francisco, California. He spent the last twenty-two years of his life in a house near the Pacific Ocean in Carmel, California.

One of Ansel's former students bought several lots in Carmel Highlands and hoped to entice other artists to join him there. He was planning to build a home for himself on one lot and wanted Ansel to build next door. Ansel resisted. He did not want to give up his splendid and familiar San Francisco setting. He was finally persuaded to make the move when he found the view in Carmel just as striking as the view he would leave behind.

The architect designed a combination house and studio to take advantage of the ocean view. In 1962, after he and Virginia were settled in the house, Ansel made it a habit to stop work in the late afternoons so that he could meet with students and friends to discuss their photographic projects and problems. He also looked forward to watching the sun set over the ocean. He often said dusk was his favorite time of day and swore that he saw a "green flash" at the exact moment when the sun slipped past the horizon. He asked Virginia and his assistants to watch with him. One of his assistants thought she saw the flash once, but she was never certain.

Opposite: *Point Sur, Storm, Big Sur, California, circa 1950*

The house was always full of flowers — tall amaryllis, white orchids along the window ledge, a bunch of nasturtiums from Virginia's garden. A dark curving fossil, an ammonite that Ansel had brought back from Utah, sat on the coffee table, bringing inside another sign of the natural world. The gallery walls off the living room were hung with his own photographs.

Ansel and Virginia in their home, Carmel Highlands, California, 1975 (Alan Ross)

Ansel spent his Carmel years teaching and lecturing, working on books of photographs, and writing technical how-to books. He promised to give his prints to the Center for Creative Photography at the University of Arizona, so that photographers and other researchers could continue to learn from his work.

Ansel was happiest when he worked. He rarely took time off. If the family took trips, they were planned around Ansel's projects. He was not content to sit on the beach and relax. He needed to be working.

But he was by no means a solitary person. During the day he spent long hours in the darkroom, but when he emerged, he was ready to be with people. He also kept in touch by writing long, detailed letters to his friends.

In his lifetime, he wrote more than one hundred thousand letters, notes, and cards. He said that the best time for him to write was early in the morning when he was still in bed, his small portable typewriter on his stomach. With two fingers, he tapped out his thoughts about his work, his travels, his worries. His letters were long, often five or six typewritten pages. He thought of them as conversations with friends.

THERE WERE MANY celebrations in the Carmel area for Ansel's eightieth birthday, including three major photographic exhibits that opened on February 19, 1982. The next night there was an elaborate dinner at the Santa Catalina School in Monterey, with speeches, toasts, and an award from the French con-

Half Dome, Winter, from Glacier Point, Yosemite National Park, circa 1940

sul. Just when Ansel thought the festivities were ending, he heard music. Drums, trombones, tubas! An eighty-piece marching band strutted in. But that was not all. Next came a birthday cake. Not an ordinary birthday cake, but a chocolate cake in the shape of Half Dome, with eighty blazing candles. Ansel took a huge breath and blew out all the candles.

Ansel with his eightieth birthday cake (Jim Alinder)

His favorite gift was the electronic horn his staff had installed in his car. He drove around Carmel, selecting from several tunes he could play, such as "When the Saints Go Marching In" and "I'm a Yankee Doodle Dandy," to startle all the bystanders.

Virginia planned another surprise for Ansel. He could not play the piano with the same ability he had as a younger man because of his gnarled, arthritic fingers. But she knew someone who could. She invited the famous pianist Vladimir Ashkenazy to play a private concert for Ansel at the house. When Ashkenazy requested she rent a Steinway piano because Ansel's Mason and Hamlin was too delicate, the secret was out. But when Ashkenazy came to practice a few days before the concert, Ansel was thrilled. He and the rest of the staff hid themselves all around the house and studio, listening and getting very little photographic work done until after the concert was held on April 29, 1982.

After the concert Ansel and Ashkenazy corresponded with each other and the musician occasionally came to visit and play carefully on Ansel's vintage piano.

Two years later Ashkenazy asked to come back again to play another concert, and the date was set for a Sunday in April. But this time Ansel was ill in the hospital, due to congestive heart failure. He insisted the concert should be held even though he could not be there. That afternoon Ashkenazy played at the house and then rushed to the hospital to see his friend and to bring him a tape of his latest recording, Brahms's Second Piano Concerto. Ansel enjoyed his visit with Ashkenazy, Virginia, and the children that afternoon.

Later that evening, while listening to the tape of Ashkenazy playing Brahms's plaintive concerto, Ansel had a fatal heart attack. He died on Easter Sunday, April 22, 1984, while listening to piano music he loved.

There is no longer an "Ansel Adams loose somewhere in this world of ours," as his mentor Alfred Stieglitz wished him to be, but his images still exist in sharp black-and-white — his mountains and waterfalls, his moons and cloudy skies, his trees in sunlight and snow. They are seen in books, in museums, in galleries, and on calendars and cards.

During his lifetime Ansel traveled all around the country taking photographs. To Yosemite, to the High Sierra, to a small cemetery in New Mexico, to an erupting geyser in Yellowstone, to a glacier in Alaska. He climbed the high peaks, lugging his camera and equipment to bring back nature's wonders.

Many would agree with what he once said: "It is easy to take a photograph, but it is harder to make a masterpiece in photography than in any other art medium." There is no question that Ansel Adams made numerous masterpieces in his long life, while at the same time managing to preserve the land he loved.

He never tried to explain his photographs, only the methods he used to take them. He left the interpretation of his images to his viewers.

Since Ansel Adams's death in 1984, young and old have lined up to see his photographs when they are exhibited in museums and galleries, and it would seem that his popularity increases with the passing years. This is a fitting tribute to the continuing relevance and power his photographs hold.

Ansel Adams made great photographs about the American wilderness; he worked tirelessly to exhibit and publish these photographs; and he made photographs not for specific environmental purposes, but as art. Unlike nearly all "environmental photographs," Ansel's were of nature untrammeled — rather than of clear-cuts and eroded hillsides and ruined streams. He sought to inspire rather than shock, because he believed deeply in beauty, and because he always spoke to the positive in humanity rather than the negative.

Ansel was an important artist because he did not photograph subjects exactly as they appeared, but rather as he saw them. He had an unparalleled inner vision and an intuitive and emotional sense of form and light. His photographs are great not because of monumental subject matter, but because he took the grandeur of nature in its simplest forms — mountains, clouds, streams, even rocks and tree stumps — and added his magic to create *art*.

Base of West Arch, Rainbow Bridge National Monument, Utah, 1942

Ansel Adams and the
Development of Photography

✳ ✳ ✳

By 1839, THREE EUROPEANS — Louis Daguerre, Joseph-Nicéphore Niepce, and William Henry Fox Talbot — had independently developed a way to make images that would not disappear. With their inventions, photography became a reality. At first, photography was immensely popular for taking family portraits. Then it was used to imitate painting, until it gradually became accepted as an art form on its own almost one hundred years later.

When Ansel Adams began taking photographs of Yosemite in 1916, he was young and so was photography. His first camera was a Kodak Box Brownie. Through the years he tried dozens of different cameras, from a heavy 8 x 10–inch wooden camera that used glass plates, to a small 35mm camera, and even a Polaroid camera that gave him immediate results.

Before he took a photograph, he visualized the scene as he expected it to look. Then he put his camera away, got out his "battered notebook, [and found] a convenient rock, stump, or fender to lean upon." On his exposure chart he recorded film speed, lens, filter, shutter speed, zone number, and any suggestions for developing the print in the darkroom.

In addition to his ability to visualize a scene, his ability in the darkroom helped him become a master photographer.

Opposite: *Lake McDonald, Glacier National Park, Montana, 1942*

Over the years he experimented with the paper, the chemicals, and the other materials he used in order to make the finest prints possible. "I know from experience that there are no shortcuts to excellence," he said.

Although Ansel is famous for his black-and-white photographs, people often wonder whether he did work with color photography. He worked in color starting in the mid-1940s and eventually made more than three thousand color transparencies, mainly on assignment for commercial projects. However, he did not develop the transparencies himself and felt that he could not control color in the same way he could his black-and-white work. Because color prints, transparencies, and negatives were subject to extensive fading over time, Ansel and most of his peers did not feel that color was a reliable form of art photography. Ansel admitted that if he had been a young man when computers first enabled artists to manipulate color photography, he certainly would have explored its possibilities more fully.

Important Dates

1902 Born February 20, San Francisco, California

1906 San Francisco earthquake, April 18

1914 Teaches himself to read music and play piano

1915 Attends Panama-Pacific Exposition

1916 Takes first trip to Yosemite; makes first photographs

1920 Appointed custodian of LeConte Memorial Lodge, Yosemite

1926 Makes first portfolio of photographs, *Parmelian Prints of the High Sierras*

1927 Takes first trip to Southwest — Santa Fe, New Mexico

1928 Marries Virginia Best in Yosemite National Park, January 2

1933 Meets Alfred Stieglitz at An American Place

Son, Michael, born August 1

1934 Elected to Board of Sierra Club; serves for thirty-seven years

1935 Daughter, Anne, born March 8

Publishes first technique book, *Making a Photograph*

1936 Has one-man exhibition at An American Place

1943 Begins Manzanar project

1946 Founds the country's first department of photography at California School of Fine Arts, San Francisco

1955 Produces, with Nancy Newhall, the conservation exhibit *This Is the American Earth*

1962 Moves from San Francisco to Carmel, California

1979 Exhibits *Ansel Adams and the West* at New York's Museum of Modern Art

1980 Receives Presidential Medal of Freedom

1984 Dies April 22, Carmel, California

Notes

Prologue

Page xi   "never the…mood." *Yosemite and the High Sierra.* Andrea G. Stillman, editor. Little, Brown and Company, 1994, across from plate 20. [*Yosemite*]

   "climb thousands…it;" Ibid., p. 130.

Page xii "staggering view…Dome" *Ansel Adams, An Autobiography.* (Boston: Little, Brown and Company, 1985), [*Autobiography*], p. 8.

Chapter 1

Page 2   Earthquakes are measured on a mathematical scale called the Richter scale. The Richter scale is not like the linear scale used in everyday measurement. Each unit of increase on the Richter scale tells you that the ground movement has increased by a factor of ten. For example, in an earthquake of magnitude 6.0, the ground moves ten times farther than in an earthquake of magnitude 5.0. In an earthquake of magnitude 7.0, the ground moves 10 x 10, or 100, times farther than in a 5.0 earthquake. Courtesy, San Francisco Exploratorium.

Page 3   "pointing violently to the left" *Autobiography,* p. 8.

Page 4   "close calls…horses." Ibid., p. 10.

Page 6   The Golden Gate Bridge was not completed until 1937.

Page 7   "Does God…young'un!" Mary Street Alinder, *Ansel Adams: A Biography* (New York: Henry Holt, 1996), p. 13. [*Biography*]

Chapter 2

Page 11   "was installed…cottage." *Autobiography,* p. 27.

Chapter 3

Page 17 In Latin, *camera obscura* means "dark room." For centuries people tried to find ways to view and reproduce images. They constructed a box or darkened a room leaving one small hole. The light that passed through the hole produced an inverted image on the wall. It was possible to trace that image on paper. John P. Schaefer, *The Ansel Adams Guide, Basic Techniques of Photography, Book 1.* (Boston, New York, London: Little, Brown and Company, 1999), p. 6. [*Guide*]

Page 19 "two thousand…miles." *Biography,* p. 20.

Page 20 "One wonder…us;" *Autobiography,* p. 53.

"Films are…already." *Ansel Adams: Letters and Images,* 1916–1984. (Boston: Little, Brown and Company, 1988.), p. 1, letter, 6/23/16. [*Letters*]

Page 22 "Yosemite…me!" *Autobiography,* p. 54.

Page 24 "make a…diary." Ibid., p. 69.

"How different…Yosemite." *Autobiography,* p. 67.

The Sierra Nevada is one of the highest and steepest mountain ranges in North America, extending north into Canada and south into Mexico. It is over four hundred miles long.

Chapter 4

Page 27 "I could see…good." Nancy Newhall, *Ansel Adams: The Eloquent Light* (New York: Aperture Inc., 1980), p. 31. [*Eloquent*]

In Mr. Dittman's darkroom Ansel learned two separate techniques:

He developed new rolls of film

    1. film rolls hung from wooden rods, 36 rolls in all

    2. lowered into 25-gallon developing tank for 5–7 minutes

    3. short-stop tank

    4. washed 20 minutes

    5. hung rod on brackets

    6. heated in drying cabinet

    7. cut films into separate frames

He made prints

    1. exposed negatives onto photographic paper

    2. developed prints in a dilute developer 3 minutes

    3. acid stop bath

    4. fixing bath 3 minutes

    5. drum washer

    6. ferrotyping solution, drained before and after

    7. heated drum dryer

Page 27 "Ansel's darkroom could have been a surgery" Interview, William Turnage.

"pure science…flourishes." Ansel Adams, *The Negative: Exposure and Development* (Hastings-on-Hudson, New York: Morgan & Morgan, Inc., 1971), p. 67. [*Negative*]

Negative 1 was rocked every ten seconds during development; negative 2 was not rocked at all; negative 3 was rocked constantly.

Page 29 "Photographers are...scores." *Autobiography*, p. 360.

"to interpret...water." Ibid., pp. 71–2.

Page 30 "moment of wonder." *The Portfolios of Ansel Adams.* (Boston: Little, Brown and Company, 1997), unpaged, Portfolio Three.

Page 32 Hutchings's book, written fifty years earlier, also called the mountains the High Sierras. It's possible that Ansel may not have realized it was incorrect the first time he read it.

Chapter 5

Page 35 "Sierra Sky and Stone." *Autobiography*, p. 143.

"To explore...Coast." *Biography*, p. 282.

"Won't it...seeing?" *Autobiography*, p. 288.

Page 36 "Literally, you...mouth." *Autobiography*, p. 144.

"my musenttuch it." *Letters*, p. 119.

"screwball theatrical productions" *Biography*, p. 100.

Page 37 "Straddlevariouses." *Autobiography*, p. 145.

"extract." Ibid., p. 145.

Page 38 "No matter...forests." Ibid., p. 143.

Page 39 "To explore, enjoy...accessible." *Biography*, p. 282.

Chapter 6

Page 41 "I was...daughter." *Autobiography*, p. 97.

"as soon...Studio." Ibid., p. 97, letter 9/5/21.

Page 43 "met someone...mother." Ibid., p. 100.

"Promise me...subjects." *Letters*, p. 21.

Page 44 "engaged-disengaged-reengaged." *Autobiography*, p. 100.

Chapter 7

Page 47 Taos Pueblo, one of the oldest Native American communities in the United States, had given Ansel permission to photograph there for as long as he needed. He decided to make original prints, rather than reproductions, to be tipped into each individual book. The finished book, *Taos Pueblo,* was published later that year. It sold for seventy-five dollars, an extremely high price for a photography book at that time, but the one hundred copies were sold out in two years. In 1980 a copy sold at auction for $12,000, and since then other copies have sold for as much as $30,000.

Page 50 "My understanding...destiny." *Autobiography*, p. 109.

Page 50 "I shall…had," *Eloquent*, p. 60, letter 10/9/31.

Page 52 "You're not…you?" *Biography*, p. 65.

Page 54 "fuzzy-wuzzies." *Autobiography*, p. 112.

On a camera, *f*-stops indicate how much light is let in through the lens, like the iris in your eye. *f*/64 is one of the smallest openings and produces a sharp image with great depth of field. *Guide*, p. 26.

Page 55 "The basic…them." *Autobiography*, p. 113.

Chapter 8

Page 57 "tough old bird." *Ansel Adams Photographer*. FilmAmerica, Inc., 1997. [Video]

Page 58 In the 1930s, there was a serious economic depression throughout the country. The stock market fell, banks failed, and many people were out of work.

"What do…two-thirty," *Autobiography*, p. 124.

Page 59 "You are…seen." *Eloquent*, p. 85.

"It is…stuff." *Autobiography*, p. 125.

"pretty snooty…up." Video.

Page 62 "You have…workmanship." *Autobiography*, p. 151.

Chapter 9

Pages 65-67 Without his light meter, Ansel had to rely on instinct and the memory of what had worked for him in the past. He knew the light value of the moon and used that to extrapolate the right aperture and exposure time. He chose *f*/32 and a one-second exposure.

Page 67 "Sometimes I…shutter!" *Eloquent*, p. 17.

Page 68 "It was…recall." *Autobiography*, p. 274.

"same phrase…head." *Eloquent*, p. 49.

"I think…best." *Letters*, p. 141.

"braiding together…luminosity." Mark Feeney, "American West: Exalted, Violated, Photographed." *Boston Globe*, Friday, March 9, 2001.

"that there…viewer." Eric Peter Nash, *Ansel Adams: The Spirit of Wild Places*. (New York: TodTri, 1995), p. 16.

Chapter 10

Page 71 "I became…regime" *Autobiography*, p. 257.

Page 73 "I think…despair" Ibid., p. 269.

Page 73 "provided the...sustenance" *Biography,* p. 237.
Page 74 "the most...do." Ibid.

Chapter 11
Page 77 "to put...perfecting" *Letters,* p. 38.
   Ansel's Zone System from *Guide,* p. 181.
Page 79 "Know what...begin!" *Autobiography,* p. 323.
   "mind's eye." Ibid., p. 320.
Page 80 "These beautiful...Sierra." *Eloquent,* p. 165, letter 12/30/38.
   "most effective... book." Ibid., p. 165, letter 12/28/38.
   "you were...ground." David Hume Kennerly, "Ansel Adams: An American Icon," ENN.com, 11/2/1999.
   Ansel applied to the Guggenheim Memorial Foundation for a grant of money that would allow him to do photographic studies of the national parks. Only advanced professionals in the arts and sciences are qualified to apply for such grants. Guggenheim Fellowships are not available to students or institutions.
Pages 82–83 "At one...institution." *Autobiography,* p. 348.

Chapter 12
Page 91 "Ansel Adams...ours." *Autobiography,* p. 203.
   "It is...medium." Ibid., p. 327.

Afterword
Page 95 "battered notebook...upon." *Eloquent,* p. 18.
Page 96 "I knew...excellence." *Guide,* p. 281.

Sources

Adams, Ansel. *An Autobiography.* Boston: Little, Brown and Company, 1985. With Mary Alinder. (New York Graphic Society books.)

_____. *Ansel Adams: Letters and Images, 1916–1984.* Boston: Little, Brown and Company, 1988. (New York Graphic Society books.)

_____. *The Negative: Exposure and Development.* Hastings-on-Hudson, New York: Morgan & Morgan, Inc., 1971.

_____. *The Portfolios of Ansel Adams.* Boston: Little, Brown and Company, 1977. (1998; 1981 Trustees of The Ansel Adams Publishing Rights Trust.)

_____. *Sierra Nevada: The John Muir Trail.* Berkeley: The Archetype Press, 1938.

_____. *Yosemite and the High Sierra.* Andrea G. Stillman, editor. Little, Brown and Company, 1994.

Alinder, Mary Street. *Ansel Adams: A Biography.* New York: Henry Holt, 1996.

Conrat, Maisie and Richard. *Executive Order 9066: The Internment of 110,000 Japanese Americans.* California Historical Society, 1972.

Nash, Eric Peter. *Ansel Adams: The Spirit of Wild Places.* New York: TodTri, 1995.

Newhall, Nancy. *Ansel Adams: The Eloquent Light. His Photographs and The Classic Biography.* New York: Aperture, Inc. 1980.

Quinn, Karen E. *Ansel Adams: The Early Years.* Boston: Museum of Fine Arts, 1991.

Schaefer, John P. *The Ansel Adams Guide. Book 1. Basic Techniques of Photography.* Boston, New York, London: Little, Brown and Company, 1999.

Sierra. January/February 2002. Vol. 87, No. 1.

Spaulding, Jonathan. *Ansel Adams and the American Landscape.* Berkeley, Los Angeles, London: UC Press, 1995.

Szarkowski, John. *Ansel Adams at 100.* Boston, New York, London: Little, Brown and Company, 2001.

Editors of Time-Life Books. *Light and Film.* Virginia: Time-Life Books, 1981.

Wolfe, Linnie Marsh. *Son of the Wilderness: The Life of John Muir.* Madison: The University of Wisconsin Press, 1945, renewed 1973.

Other References:

Feeney, Mark. "American West: Exalted, Violated, Photographed." *Boston Globe,* Friday, March 9, 2001.

Videotape: *Ansel Adams Photographer.* FilmAmerica, Inc., 1997. Best's Studio, Inc.

Internet: Kennerly, David Hume. "Ansel Adams: An American Icon." ENN.com, 11/2/1999.

Interview: Rick Knepp, Weston Gallery, 1/5/2001.

Telephone interview: Mary Alinder, 11/30/2000.

Acknowledgments

The author wishes to thank the following
for their help in providing images for the book:

Claudia Kishler, The Ansel Adams Publishing Rights Trust

Leslie Calmes and Dianne Nilsen, The Center for Creative Photography,
The University of Arizona

Selby Collins, San Francisco History Center

Ellen Byrne, William E. Colby Memorial Library

Susan Snyder, Bancroft Library

Anthony Montoya, Paul Strand Archive

David and Myrna Wright, Bodega Bay

David Stanhope, Jimmy Carter Library

Jim Alinder, Alinder Galleries

Beverly and Jack Wilgus, The Wilgus Collection

* ***** *

All images other than those listed below are reprinted with the permission of The Ansel Adams
Publishing Rights Trust.

Page 4: *Children in refugee camp after San Francisco earthquake, 1906.* Courtesy of the San Francisco History
Center, San Francisco Public Library.

12: *Constructing the Aeroscope at the Panama-Pacific Exposition, 1915.* Courtesy of the San Francisco History
Center, San Francisco Public Library.

13: *Car transporting the public through the Exposition grounds, 1915.* Courtesy of the San Francisco History Center, San Francisco Public Library.

14: *Ansel's eighth-grade diploma.* Copyright © The Center for Creative Photography, The University of Arizona.

17: *Illustration of a man using a portable camera obscura to trace an image projected from the outside world.* Copyright © Bright Bytes Studio. From the collection of Jack and Beverly Wilgus.

22: *Entrance to Camp Curry, Yosemite National Park.* Courtesy of the San Francisco History Center, San Francisco Public Library.

35: *Ansel with wooden camera and tin cup, 1930s (Cedric Wright).* Courtesy of William E. Colby Memorial Library, Sierra Club. Reprinted by permission of David Wright.

36: *Hundreds of Sierra Club hikers around a campfire at Darwin Bench, 1950s (Cedric Wright).* Courtesy of the Bancroft Library, University of California, Berkeley. Reprinted by permission of David Wright.

42: *Virginia Rose Best and Merced River, Yosemite National Park, circa 1921 (Ansel Adams).* Courtesy of Jeanne and Michael Adams.

45: *Ansel measuring photographs of Yosemite with Michael looking on, circa 1935.* Courtesy of the San Francisco History Center, San Francisco Public Library.

51: *Iris, Maine, 1928 (Paul Strand).* Copyright © Aperture Foundation, Inc., Paul Strand Archive.

73: *Grandfather and grandchildren awaiting evacuation bus (Dorothea Lange).* Courtesy of the Bancroft Library, University of California, Berkeley.

82: *Ansel receiving the Presidential Medal of Freedom from President Carter, Washington, D.C., 1980.* Courtesy of the Jimmy Carter Library.

90: *Ansel with his eightieth birthday cake (Jim Alinder).* Reprinted by permission of the photographer.

112: *Ansel Adams, 1976 (Arnold Newman).* Copyright © Arnold Newman / Getty Images. Reprinted by permission.

Index

Ansel Adams, 1976 (© Arnold Newman | Getty Images)

Many thanks to Bill Turnage, of The Ansel Adams Publishing Rights Trust,
for the many hours he devoted to sharing his memories of
Ansel and to shaping this book to honor him.

DESIGNED BY

Alyssa Morris

PRODUCTION COORDINATED BY

Linda Jackson and Sandra Klimt

SEPARATIONS BY

Thomas Palmer

PAPER IS

150 gsm Gardamatt

ENGRAVED, PRINTED, AND BOUND BY

Amilcare Pizzi, Milan, Italy

TEXT IS

Spectrum

DISPLAY TYPE IS

Opti Deligne and Lord Swash